Carole A...

You are a beautiful Soul

Trust Your Intuition
Your Protector
Your Guide

Lots of Love & Light

YVONNE J DOUGLAS

DEDICATION

I dedicate this book to my sisters Sharon, Sonia, Sandra and Kayla

CONTENTS

ACKNOWLEDGMENTS

I would like to thank all the people that have been placed on my path to help me grow and learn and become the person I am today.

Thank you to all my soul sisters – too many to mention but you know you have touched me in one way or another.

Thanks to Anita, Karen, Mary Jane, Clare, Melanie, Jackie, Maureen, Jennifer (Khat), Sherry Ann, Suneet, & Tanya blessed love to you all.
Thanks you Rowan Campus for your contributions and for the front cover. Thank you Jonathon for listening

Thank you to Lorraine and Angela my two wonderful, inspiring, loving and supportive mentors and friends.

Thank you to my family members who continue to support me and to my long time loyal friends.

Thank you to my wonderful children who teach me so much. I admire you both for your courage and love and as always I love you dearly.

FOREWORD

By Lorraine Murray

When instinct, intuition, common sense etc. contradicts our idealistic and subjective views of personal happiness and contentment, we find it easier to gravitate to an unexplainable confused mode rather than follow our instinct. It happens to the best of us; even those who are qualified to counsel others on the subject. So why are some people more susceptible to intuition paralysis in relationships than others?

I met Yvonne about 10 years ago whilst working in the Investment Banking Industry and we have been friends ever since. Most people find it difficult to admit they have made a mistake, especially in relationships. I admire Yvonne for having the courage to share those mistakes with us in order to allow others to increase wisdom and be in a position to recognise 'real' happiness and contentment. Although subtle, it is evident that Yvonne is empowering the reader to take control of their future and long-term happiness by embracing the power of intuition.

Yvonne describes intuition as our sixth sense, a personal gift from God, which we risk losing to alternatives; naivety and ignorance. Yvonne masterfully captures her journey from naivety to enlightenment in bite-size stages that enable the reader to absorb the learning at a comfortable pace. The author is considerate of the fact that she is taking you on a journey that you may not be comfortable with. Yvonne assists the reader to recognise when and why we ignore our intuition and provides the tools for corrective action.

Throughout the chapters the author openly shares personal experiences and professional knowledge surrounding intimacy, selective hearing and understanding, what is said vs what is meant etc., in a way that is relative and endears the author to the reader.

The book supplements that sensible friend we all have and love; a trusted person of integrity who remains rational in a crisis. We call this friend when we want our intuition to be re-affirmed, despite the possibility of receiving a reprimand for questioning the intuition. This book provides the advice you need, at a pace you set, without the threat of a reprimand!

The book, Trust Your Intuition, is also cleverly and uniquely structured to incorporate workshop material, thereby giving the reader the opportunity to document and self-assess their own examples of where they have been more/less effective in leveraging their instinct.

If the objective of this book is to assist the reader to minimise future mistakes and pain resulting from ignoring intuition, Yvonne has certainly achieved that and more. As you read through each chapter, it is evident Yvonne has an unyielding passion and determination to make a positive intervention in people's lives.

This is a truly sincere and inspirational journey for the reader to enjoy and embrace. If you want to establish proactive good relationships, as opposed to retrospective bad relationships, I encourage you to invest in this book; it will not disappoint!

Lorraine Murray

CONTACT

If you would like to get in touch with Yvonne for her services you may reach her through the following means:

www.onenessofspirit.co.uk
www.yvonnejdouglas.com
+44 203674 1571
+44 741583 4579

INTRODUCTION

The instinct of a woman is what keeps her safe from harm. It is an in built compass that will always be there and has always been there. It will help her make some of the most serious decisions she will ever have to make. It was and always has been part of her make-up. The instinct or intuition is a powerful sense and connects her to her higher self and God. To deny yourself of the sixth sense is to deny your connection to God and the universe. A woman in touch with her intuition is a formidable force. Within it lies one of her greatest powers. To follow your intuition is to follow his universal will for you. God is well pleased when you do so. The more you follow it the more you will prosper.

However so many do not trust their intuition, why is this? This is because they are cut off from its connection. They may also have trust issues stemming from some trauma they may have undergone. In addition they are not taught the importance of it from a young age. Just as the animals live with instinct so do we as humans. This society has a lot to answer for in contributing to the demise of the female intuition. The connection to the most high and the universe is a woman's strength and power. Now is the time for women to rise up and connect and as their divine energies connect the world will begin to change. The world around us will start to protect us. The energy field around the globe will become more loving, more nurturing, less aggressive, less competitive and it will be a blissful state for earths inhabitants.

One way to heal is to reconnect to the universal creator, that connection to higher self is the same connection to the universal creator and it is that connection that brings about true happiness. This is where happiness lives. Nothing outside of you brings you true happiness.

The connection allows you to access information coming from a higher source. Things you know intuitively and you wonder where the information came from. You surprise yourself with what may come flying out of your mouth. That is intuitive knowledge coming from above. By keeping your mind and body pure you can access this information that you instinctively know. Quiet your mind and listen to the messages. Get yourself some quiet time on a regular basis and hear, see and feel the messages coming through. We are not taught about our sixth sense for a reason, it was done to keep us in darkness, so to speak. However, we came from the darkness and within it there is light and knowledge. When you close your eyes and meditate, what do you see? Yes it is dark, but you can access information from the universe as your intuition speaks to you.

It is important to remember the necessity of staying connected. That connection will allow you to prosper because the vibration is a high frequency vibration. It is in harmony with the universe; the abundant universe.

"The War on Men Through the Degradation of Woman" –

"How is man to recognize his full self, his full power through the eyes of an incomplete woman? The woman who has been stripped of Goddess recognition and diminished to a big ass and full breast for physical comfort only. The woman who has been silenced so she may forget her spiritual essence because her words stir too much thought outside of the pleasure space. The woman who has been diminished to covering all that rots inside of her with weaves and red bottom shoes.

I am sure the men, who restructured our societies from cultures that honored woman, had no idea of the outcome. They had no idea that eventually, even men would render themselves empty and longing for meaning, depth and connection.

There is a deep sadness when I witness a man that can't recognize the emptiness he feels when he objectifies himself as a bank and truly believes he can buy love with things and status. It is painful to witness the betrayal when a woman takes him up on that offer.

He doesn't recognize that the [creation] of a half woman has contributed to his repressed anger and frustration of feeling he is not enough. He then may love no woman or keep many half women . as his prize.

He doesn't recognize that it's his submersion in the imbalanced warrior culture, where violence is the means of getting respect and power, as the reason he can break the face of the woman who bore him four children.

When woman is lost, so is man. The truth is, woman is the window to a man's heart and a man's heart is the gateway to his soul. Power and control will NEVER outweigh love. May we all find our way.

~ Jada Pinkett-Smith, Sinuous Magazine ~

Yvonne J Douglas

PART 1

1 QUESTIONS

Two years ago I published my first book. Over 2.5 years ago, I met who I thought was the man of my dreams. He made me laugh; he made me feel safe and secure. He supported me and he restored my faith in men, so I thought.

What happened? Yes, what really happened? I was not seeing reality as laid before my eyes. Why was I so blinded? Was I desperate to have a man? I don't think so. But maybe, just maybe I was desperate to make a relationship work. After all, wouldn't you, if you had gone through two failed marriages?

What happened? Everything seemed so blissful. But maybe I was lying to myself a little. I saw the signs but thought no-one is perfect, slowly but surely I allowed myself to be controlled and manipulated.

How? I am smart, I'm a counsellor; how the hell did I allow this to happen? You know how, I did not listen to my intuition, not really. Or maybe I didn't quite trust it. In all honesty I think I was not sure if it was my women's intuition or just me being fearful of opening up to love. In the end I resigned myself to the fact that it was fear and I was sabotaging my future happiness. Confused? Yeah, so am I, or should I say, so was I?

I was told by him that a woman's intuition isn't always right, some get it wrong. That sentence made me sit up and think and all my suspicions were confirmed. By this time I had already made up my mind to leave him, so for him to tell me that was futile. By then I had learned to trust my intuition and not ignore it. So today, as I write these words I pledge never to ignore my intuition ever again. It is so strong at times that I do not know how the hell I could have ignored it.

This book is a continuation of my life focusing on a woman's intuition, or for men, their gut instinct. Man or woman we all have that sixth sense that they do not teach us about in school. That's another story, or book!! Your intuition or instinct is as real as your sight. It is an extension of all our other senses in an extremely heightened form. It is that *feeling* you get that tells you not to go down that particular road because it is not safe; when you *feel* someone standing close behind you; when you *sense* someone is lying to you.

You see, we are energy and we are all connected hence why the above is possible. We can walk past someone and feel negative or positive energy emitting from that person. We are more than just our physical bodies, we also have a etheric body, astral body, mental body, spiritual body, astral body and the soul.

Oftentimes we use hindsight to learn from bad experiences and we wish that we had foresight because foresight would save us from experiencing certain situations. Well, we do have foresight and it is just a matter of being connected, trusting what we sense and listening to our intuition. Would you not be so much happier learning from foresight rather than hindsight?

I will be using examples of couples I know and some of my own experiences to help identify this area of a woman's life, especially in terms of her relationship with her partner, lover or spouse. Please join me on this journey and learn how you will never again be misled by others, because you trust your intuition. Even though I use examples of women needing to trust their intuition, my examples can equally be applied for men when it comes to women. This book is not about being anti-men; I am writing it from a woman's perspective.

Learn how you can trust your intuition so that you will no longer put up with being manipulated, exploited, deceived and emotionally abused in any way shape or form; by partners, friends, employers, family, even the good old sales person. Learn how to discover the goddess or god within. Learn how to become a fully empowered being by following and trusting your intuition. Finally, learn how to embrace yourself as a sexual being without fear of judgment.

2 MORE THERAPY

So I am experiencing a relationship like I have never experienced before. I am no longer using food to cushion my feelings and all that I have learnt I am applying in my relationship. I am open to being vulnerable, this is new territory for me, but I am willing to give it a go. I want to test my ability to sustain a relationship and be successful. When I met my partner it was only a few months after I realised that I had been sexually abused by my stepfather David. My recovered memory had finally brought it all to light. Yes it freaked me out which sent me back into therapy in order to deal with it. To make matters worse, he had passed away which meant I was not able to confront him. So here I am with this anger and hurt not knowing what to do with it.

I have more therapy which helps me to process what is

going on for me and helps me in my relationship. I start to explore my identity as a woman living in a male dominated society. I even look at my identity as a black woman living is a society that is quite covertly racist. Included in my exploration is how my past beliefs as a Jehovah's Witness had an impact on me and my identity. I was feeling somewhat confused and oh so vulnerable.

My relationship was quite taxing too. I was analysing so many of the things that were going on. Was I sabotaging the relationship? Was he sabotaging it? Why were things so tense a lot of the time? I had so many questions that needed answering. All this was surprising for me because I thought that I had everything sorted. Why was everything so challenging? Couldn't I just live happily ever after?

I did rely heavily on my partner and him on me. We did so much together and saw each other very often. I felt as if he was there for me and I wanted to be there for him too. Our relationship was quite intense.

3 ISSUES WITH SEX

In the early stages I remember sex being quite difficult for me which surprised me somewhat. I actually felt as if I was being raped at times. Don't get me wrong my partner was never forceful or anything like that. But I was having flashbacks during sex. There were times that I would go into panic mode and felt ever so afraid, it was as if he was violating me and many times I had to stop. Luckily I was able to explain to my partner what was happening for me and he understood. He helped me to see that it was just a memory or a feeling and that I should focus heavily on the present moment and not the past. So whenever we got intimate in that way I would have to repeat over and over again in my head who I was with and that I was safe. It was a great technique and after some months I finally started to feel safe with my partner.

In addition I went to see an energy healer as I felt that I was all talked out with talking therapy. I still had stuff to release and my body was hanging onto pain and memories. You see, as much I realised that I had been abused before I could even talk the memories was not vivid. However, my body remembered the trauma and it was still stuck in my body. I was becoming anxious and tired. I felt as if my issues would never go away and wondered whether I should have even opened Pandora's Box; however, something inside told me to keep going.

I was a little apprehensive about seeing an energy healer, it wasn't something I was used to, I also didn't know much about it and I wasn't sure if all this energy thing would even work. However, I had heard good things about it and thought I had nothing to lose. So I called the young woman in question. She was also an intuitive reader and as soon as I got on the phone with her she started to tell me that I needed to stop thinking so much and that I needed to go for a walk. How odd I thought. I was rather impressed at how she knew what was going on for me, she even picked up on the fact that I still had unresolved issues around my mother, which actually surprised me but later turned out to be true. I couldn't wait to see this woman.

So I book my appointment to see her for some energy healing. I find my way to her premises and am greeted and welcomed. I sit there a little nervous but keen to get going. After she takes some notes I hop onto her couch and am told to lie down, close my eyes and just relax. She has very soft relaxing music playing in the background and essential oils burning. Before long she starts her process. As she moves around I start to relax more and more but at some points I start to feel ever so emotional, I even see red lights flashing before my eyes. This stuff is weird, I think to myself. After a while I think I can hear myself snoring and before long I am woken up by the young lady. We compare notes of what she could see energy wise and what was going on for me at certain times. The pain in my left arm corresponded to the unresolved issues with my mother and there was pain in my right arm also, which meant I still had issues on my paternal side. My biological father or my step-father, probably both, I thought. I was advised to write a therapeutic letter to my mother. That night I slept really well.

Even though I had already done this some years back, I

wrote another letter to my mother and burned it; the pain in my left arm disappeared. I was sold on this energy healing, and couldn't wait for my follow up appointment.

Subsequent visits proved even more powerful. I remember crying when she worked around my womb area, I was certainly releasing some emotional pain. I started to feel stronger, safer, empowered and sensual and it felt liberating.

4 ENLIGHTENMENT

As I started to feel stronger my relationship began to change, which is inevitable as nothing really stays the same. This caused a strain on our relationship because my partner was not developing at the same rate. The relationship became unevenly yoked. In fact, I got to a point where I was dealing with more and more of my issues that kept coming up and as this was happening I was becoming more reliant on myself and my intuition. However, I felt as if I was being paranoid within the relationship.

Was I going mad, or was what I was feeling, dreaming, thinking true and real? Needless to say as time went on I was becoming more doubtful about my relationship. However, I was not feeling brave enough to end it; I was determined to make it work. But it takes two to make it work. I became quite frantic as things were not adding up. I started questioning things; I was even told that since seeing the intuitive reader that I had changed, he felt it was for the worse. But the reality was that I was getting stronger, speaking and owning my truth more.

Even a beautiful holiday abroad did not fix things, it felt like it did at first but within a month things came to a head. However, I did not fully trust my instinct. I spoke to another intuitive reader and she told me what I needed to hear, but more importantly she told me these words that rang so loudly in my head I could not ignore them, she said " you are very very intuitive, but you do not listen". At that point I felt somewhat empowered. I started to go back and think about all the little incidents that did not add up and how I felt and how I did not follow through on that feeling. There were so many incidents that I had ignored, that I started to feel as if I had let myself down immensely. I started to feel sick, angry and hurt.

So here I am now in a relationship that is going nowhere fast. Coming to this realisation was not easy however; I had to be true to myself I had to trust my intuition for once in my life. I did and I ended it, I felt relieved and free. Don't get me wrong, it hurt real bad, I went through the angry stage, the sad stage, the denial and the lonely stage and then finally the acceptance. It took me a good eight months to get over completely but in those eight months let me tell you what I did.

My personal development was my main focus. Embracing my spiritual side was imperative. I remembered about three years ago an aura soma therapist told me I had spiritual gifts but it was blocked due to food. You see, unhealthy foods can block our connection to source. It certainly did mine and I did not even realise how much weight I had put on whilst in the relationship. So many issues were triggered in it because it was not really a healthy relationship, this is what I realised even more in hindsight. How much better is foresight hey? So as I said, the reason why I wised up toward the end of the relationship was because I got more of a handle on my food. I started to 'see'.

Within six months of focusing on my healing, my spiritual and personal development, I embraced my intuitive abilities and. Firstly I went on a website and took the online test, the results were astounding, from my answers the test concluded that I had many spiritual gifts with my strongest one being clairsentient and claircognizant. I then started to practice using Angel cards. To my amazement I was accurate; this was exciting times for me. I started to read many spiritual books incessantly learning all about this new world. There was so much I did not know, so much to learn. I was also enjoying life, enjoying being me. I started to feel really connected to God and the Universe, it felt like nothing I had ever felt before (or could remember feeling). It dawned on me that I felt truly happy and I was on a natural and spiritual high. It felt fantastic. I was being authentic, I was accepting myself fully.

My appetite for learning about this part of me was huge and I continued reading, and learning. Going to different groups and practicing. I have met some amazing soul sisters along the way, showing me that I am definitely on the right path it all felt like I was living on a different vibrational plane.

So this is why I write this book, to help you realise the importance of trusting your intuition. It's a life saver. I would like you to go through part 2 of this book and really work through it to see how you too can really connect to your higher self and keep yourself safe from unhealthy relationships.

PART 2

5 INITIAL MEETING

The scene is set, you get dressed up making sure that you look your best, you get your hair done, nails done, and not forgetting your twinkle toes too. You want to make sure that you feel good because you know that feeling good makes the difference in how you experience your world. You're out with your friends and you are having a wonderful time, you're letting your hair down for the first time in ages. You have been single for a while and you feel that you are now ready to have someone enter into your life. Then he walks up to you and asks you for a dance. You politely allow him to slip his hand behind your back and draw you close to him. It has been a while since you have been so close to a man, and as you feel his warm embrace, smell his lovely aftershave and his strong manly physique standing there, holding you, you just feel so light on your feet. You wonder if this could be the one.

Come off it; get your head out of the clouds young lady. It is just a dance and you have barely said two words to him. Yes he dances well; he smells like he had a shower at some point today and yes he looks half decent. Did you check his shoes? Only kidding. Ok, so you dance for a while. Check how he is dancing with you. Is he allowing you to move into his space or is he pushing himself into your space? Is he trying to do the dirty dancing, or is he happy to do the two-step with you as you talk over the music? If he just wants to dirty dance, then he is not the one. I don't care how nice he feels, he is not the one. Deep down you know he is not the one. So, either you enjoy the dirty dancing and know that's where it ends or you take your leave after the first dance.

So ok, next…. this one is not doing the dirty dancing but talks nicely to you asking you your name and blah blah blah. Yes, this one is polite, he could be the one. Let's put the brakes on here a minute. Who said you are going to find the one in a club? Let's be serious now. It happens, but it is very rare so let us just say neither of them is going to be the one. Skip the club scene and decide that you are not going to meet the man of your dreams at the club. When you go to the club go just to enjoy yourself with the girls, let your hair down, dance your little socks off and be carefree. Dance as if you are dancing in your bedroom, well maybe not so overtly sexually, but hey, be yourself and do not worry about who is looking at you and who is wearing the same dress as you and whose shoes look bad etc.

When you do meet a man that you fancy and the feeling seems to be mutual. What feelings are you getting? Check out what is going on for you. Does he make you feel good? Do you have a nice feeling about him? Or do you have a suspicious feeling about him? Do you feel he is just a charmer? Does he seem genuine? Does he have good eye contact, or does he appear to be shifty? If you are generally not a judgmental type of person, then you can rely on your initial feelings of when you first met him. Go with those feelings.

So you go away feeling good, he has taken your number and he promises to call you.

How long do you wait for the call? One, two, three days... one week; two weeks? Would you have called him?

Well, I have been told by many men that if he likes you and is interested he will call at the very latest on the third day. If he calls after that, then he is not that into you. It could also mean that he may have liked you but is not really in a position, for whatever reason, to start getting to know you. Unfortunately for me, I waited two weeks before I contacted my ex, and when I did contact him, he was so awfully glad I called because he lost my number. We had exchanged business cards and I didn't lose his. I was outraged when I did not hear from him and spoke to friends, one was even a man and I was given the advice that anything could have happened, he could have lost his phone, lost my number blah blah blah. Oh, how I wish I had not listened to their advice, but sometimes you like to give people the benefit of the doubt. This was clear evidence that he was not really into me. But my intuition was over-ridded with justifications. As it happens, further down the line, I found my card amongst a whole load of papers in his room.

Marsha, a lovely young lady in her 30's, met Samuel and they spoke on the phone a few times before they decided to meet up. They then set a day and time for their first date. Samuel wasn't driving at the time, so he set off to meet Marsha at her home using public transport. Not a problem at all. However, it was a Sunday and he clearly did not check out bus/train times and arrived at Marsha's home nearly two hours late. When he finally arrived he assumed that they would be staying in, not even taking into consideration the fact that her children were likely to be home. Marsha had expected him to plan their date and where they would be going. No planning involved whatsoever, Marsha was not too impressed. Marsha ensured that they went out for the date and she drove them to a wine bar where they had a good night. At the end of the date Marsha drove Samuel home and they sat in the car talking for a while. Samuel invited Marsha up to his flat to watch videos. Marsha refused as she felt it was too soon, so they said their goodbyes after a little kiss and she drove herself home.

Do you agree with what Marsha had done? What would you have done? Would you have questioned him as to why he doesn't drive?

Marsha felt that the date went really well and was pleased that she did not go into his flat because she wanted him to see her as wife material. Well done Marsha! However, alarm bells are already ringing, which Marsha is ignoring. She was annoyed that he turned up late for the date, agitated that he had not planned where they were going to go and a little suspicious that he had invited her up to his flat on the first night. Intuition is speaking here; however, Marsha did not listen. She was all wrapped up in the fact that she met this new man who was attractive and yes they did have a good time.

Watch the signs from the beginning as they are a clear indication of how the relationship will be. If a new partner does not make much of an effort in the beginning can you imagine what they will be like further down the line? First impressions do count. They will test you to see what you will put up with. People with low self-esteem will be taken advantage of. If you put up with nonsense it means you have work to do on your self-esteem.

6 ARRANGING DATES

Marsha and Samuel continued to date and more often than not, Samuel was always late for anything they arranged. Marsha would get quite annoyed about this and would generally show her upset by having a strop which in turn, led Samuel to become defensive. Marsha needed to find a better way to communicate her upset.

How would you have handled the situation?

Marsha was a stickler for time and was always bang on time, if not early. Her and Samuel seemed to be out of sync, what were they to do? After many discussions it was decided that Marsha would relax a little around the time issue and Samuel would make more of an effort to be on time. Finally after many months they were pretty much in sync, give or take 10/15 minutes.

Initially the time issue really upset Marsha and she put up with it for far too long. Yes they finally compromised, but not after some really heated arguments where Samuel managed to manipulate Marsha into believing that she needed to accept the fact that they saw time differently. Marsha did not listen to her gut instinct here, she so wanted this relationship to work out so she allowed this to continue.

Should she have accepted his lateness, should it have taken so long to come to a compromise?

Now I will let you into a little secret, if a man finds it difficult to commit to meeting you at a set time on a continuous basis, then he is afraid of commitment. This is a sign that he will not commit to you in the long run. Being on time is a commitment in itself and if someone continually turns up late it says a lot not just about their commitment issues but also about their disrespect for your time. No-one's time is more important than yours. Marsha should have shown Samuel the door by now, but she so wanted the relationship to work and she worked hard at it.

In my own relationship I found that I was doing most of the calling. One particular day I waited for him to call. He had told me a couple of days before that he would call me on this particular day, however, he did not dial my digits. I was not impressed, so I sent him a message to let him know this. I was rather polite and simply stated that "When someone says they are going to call I expect them to call unless there is an emergency". Well who told me to text that? He was none too pleased and decided to ignore me, that's right, no response for hours. The following day I became rather worried and livid as I do not take kindly to being ignored. I called my friend and received some sound advice. 'Lock the psycho Yvonne in the cupboard'. So that's what I did, and took the sane Yvonne to his house. I went for two reasons, I was worried that something may have happened and I needed to know what was going on.

What would you have done?

We talked things through and managed to get back on an even keel. Now, this whole fiasco was yet another sign that I should not have been pursuing this relationship; yet again I ignored my intuition.

The following was relayed to me by someone I know; let's call her Hannah to protect her identity. She related how she was seeing her new friend for a few weeks now and she wanted to go out clubbing with her friend as her friends' boyfriend was a DJ. Hannah wanted her new man friend –

Andrew to come along and at first he agreed. Then at the last minute he said he wasn't feeling too well and he was no longer going. Hannah said she felt disappointed that he would not be able to go and felt sorry that he wasn't feeling too well. She wondered if she should still go out without him and although he said she should, there was a slight feeling in the pit of her stomach which told her that he did not want her to go out without him.

Would you have gone out without him, or would you have sacrificed your night out and gone to his house?

However, what she decided to do was go out and offered to go and see him after. He was happy for her to do that and she felt as if she was doing the right thing by her and her new man.

Hannah said that even though she was enjoying herself she felt a little guilty about being out whilst her new man wasn't feeling well and was at home resting.

Would you be feeling guilty too?

I asked her why she should feel guilty, and she could not explain herself. This is co-dependency. We will talk about that later. Anyway I was a little concerned for Hannah as she went on to talk about what took place when she left the club and made her way to see Andrew. She called his phone to let him know she was leaving the club so he would have an idea when to expect her. However, there was no answer. Hannah was a little concerned but thought it wasn't such an issue as she had told him roughly what time she would be leaving the club. She decided to still make her way to his house.

On arrival she called his phone, one, two, three times. No answer, she knocked his door, no answer, she called his phone again, no answer. Hannah could not believe what was happening. She was upset, confused and extremely angry. She had left the club early to be with him and he was not answering her call or the door. Was he even there? She thought. Hannah said, she decided to go home but she was ever so upset.

What should Hannah have done? What would you have done?

The following day, Andrew called Hannah and apologised so very nicely that he had fallen asleep. Hannah thought that was a feeble excuse and sensed something rather ominous. She knew he was expecting her and as such he would have his phone in ear shot and if he fell asleep then he would be able to hear the phone ring. Well, that is what she would have done, if the tables were turned. Even though Hannah felt this feeling, she ignored it.

Would you have ignored it and given him the benefit of the doubt?

Marsha and Samuel had an awful experience when arranging to meet up to go out for an evening. Marsha had been putting up with Samuel being continually late for their dates/meet ups. One night Marsha arrived on time as usual and Samuel was no-where near ready and did not seem to feel the need to rush. His attitude was that he has to rush to work 5 days a week so he felt no need to do the same on his time at the weekends. That's a fair point; however, it is not just his time is it?

What are you thinking? Do you agree?

On this particular occasion Marsha was very annoyed, he had not even had his shower yet. Marsha made it quite clear that she was not happy about the situation, but because she was so fed up of his constant lateness and having a somewhat lax attitude about it Marsha sulked instead of addressing it in an adult fashion. This caused Samuel to become extremely angry and interpreting Marsha's annoyance as disrespectful. Marsha described to me that Samuel became rather indignant and insisting that Marsha was being disrespectful and as his woman she should not be carrying on in this fashion.

Do you agree with Samuel? What would you have

said to Samuel if it were you?

Marsha told me that she could not believe how he behaved, she said it was as if he was throwing his toys out of the pram and turning it around on her. She felt that if anyone should be angry in this way, it was her. She told me that he was consistently late and felt that she should just put up and shut up. Marsha did not have the courage to tell him where to go, she wanted to go out and have a good time with her man. Eventually she ended up apologising to him for the way she behaved.

Would you have done the same, if not, what would you have done differently?

If you do not value yourself and your time, others will not value you or your time either. Again, start how you mean to go on.

7 LISTEN

Do you listen to when a man speaks, or do you get all wrapped up in the nice fluffy feeling of being in love? Do you get taken in by all the romance, all the nice feelings floating around in your body? That in love feeling, the excitement of a new relationship when you are floating on cloud nine; it can mess with your mind. It can make you very forgetful or it can make you hear what you want to hear. Listen when a man speaks to you. He will tell you from the beginning what he wants. Sometimes he is very clear but sometimes you also have to listen to what he does not say. Watch what he does not do. Read between the lines.

Now I remember having a conversation with my partner and we were talking about a friend who recently got engaged. I get all gooey when I hear this because when I see two people who are in love and commit to one another I think it is a beautiful thing. When he saw my response he asked me "You don't want to do all that again do you?" At that point I was not particularly bothered about marrying again. I said, "maybe although it's not a necessity".

What are you thinking right now about what he said? Do you sense anything?

Now sometime after this event about 10 months into our relationship my partner wrote a beautiful song and dedicated it to me. There was a certain part in the song that said "I see you as my wife". I was so touched by this song that it made me cry. At this point I really thought that this man was interested in marrying me. He actually said that is how he feels but he cannot do much right now due to finances. I thought that it was a fair comment and did not realise that he was full of …..

Some men are good at fooling you into believing that they have the best and same intentions as yourself this is why it is so important to listen to your intuition. It is also a very good idea to follow the 90 day rule. The 90 day rule states that you must wait for at least 90 days before having sex with your new partner. This way you are in a far better frame of mind to work them out. Sex can blur your senses and before you know it you have fallen in love or lust with someone because the sex is good. Without sex you can make a much more informed decision about whether this man is good for you. The only issue with the 90 day rule is that some men are prepared to wait, oh yes some will wait years just to get what they want. However, if you are in touch with your intuition and emotionally mature men will see this and they probably won't stick around long enough if their intentions are not genuine. Trust your intuition as to when it is the right time for you to take the relationship onto the next level, it will be different for each individual.

Hannah relayed to me a situation that had occurred between her and Andrew. Hannah loved to talk about how they first met and what it was like for her and wanted to know exactly what Andrew thought of her when they first met. When they met Hannah was dressed in a tight mini dress with leggings, looking rather sexy which clearly attracted Andrew. Andrew had made a joke that he was just going to 'hit it and run'.

What would you have thought if your partner had made that joke to you, about you?

Hannah was a little shocked at the joke, thought it was quite funny, but deep down wondered if it were really true. They had by now fallen in love and she thought that's what counted now. He convinced her that it was just a joke and he never really thought that about her. Hannah should have listened to her intuition as it was a very poignant remark which indicates what Andrew's true intentions may really have been from the start.

Save yourself from heartache later down the line by really listening to what they say and don't say. If your intuition kicks in, listen.

8 HOW DOES HE TALK ABOUT EX PARTNERS?

Now this is a very important question. Hannah reported to me that Andrew had an ex-wife who he felt was rather cold. He often called her a whore. Marsha told him that she was not comfortable with him calling the mother of his children a whore. Andrew spoke badly of his ex-wife and how awful she was as a mother and wife. Regardless of this Hannah felt it was inappropriate for him to be referring to her with such profanity. Now I don't know about you but....

What are your views on how a man talks about his ex?

This suggests at least two things; either he has not overcome the break-up of the marriage and needs to get some help. Or he has a no real respect for women. Hannah was confused because she felt Andrew treated her with respect most of the time. However, there were times when Hannah noticed that Andrew often seemed to resent women in authority, his boss for example. She also recognised that if a woman said anything to him that he did not quite like or agree with, he was often quite disrespectful in what he had to say about her. Albeit, in her eyes, he treated Hannah respectfully, this rings alarms bells. Andrew had issues with women.

Think back to past relationships, how did your ex's talk about women?

What confused Hannah was that he spoke so highly of his mother (who had passed onto the other side). He missed her very much and often spoke about her. We generally use as a benchmark how men feel about women according to their relationship with their mother. However, in this case there was conflict. He did not speak highly of women in general. How he spoke about his mother could have been because she had passed.

So be very mindful of how your partner speaks of women and their ex partners, it will give you a good indication of how they will treat you and if there are any unresolved issues.

9 CONTROL

Every woman loves it when her man buys her gifts. She feels special and spoilt. I remember going out with my ex and we were having a lovely time, talking about this, that and the other. He often mentioned how he wanted 'his woman' to dress. He felt it was important that she dressed decently. I tended to agree. However, it is important to note, that your perception of decent could well be very different to his. This was the case with me and my partner. I very much had an issue with what he expected because of how I was dressed when he met me.

So on this day out in Camden I happen to see an outfit on a mannequin and mention that I liked it. It was rather short, something that you could wear with a pair of leggings, which is how I would have worn it. My ex becomes quite angry thinking that I am not taking him seriously about his views on how a woman should dress. I was actually joking about the dress/top, but was rather concerned about his reaction. It seemed so extreme. He wanted to end the day out, sit in the car and discuss the situation. I managed to calm him down, stressing that I was only joking, although I wasn't. On that day he bought me two lovely maxi dresses.

What do you think of the above situation? Would you have said anything? Would you have accepted the dresses?

I was chuffed to be getting a present from my boyfriend and I liked the dresses – really I did. However, there was constant talk of how I dressed and at times it became tiring. It even came to the point where I said to him, "if you had your way you would have me wearing a hijab". That's how pressured I felt even though I did not give into the pressure. Because of this there was a constant battle of wills.

Marsha had similar issues with Samuel. She remembers Samuel saying that he felt quite betrayed by her because she wore a vest top out and about in the summer, 'showing off her ample breasts'. This angered and confused Marsha because before he actually told her how he felt, he switched off from her and gave her the silent treatment whilst they were in the car. She told me she did not know what the hell was going on and couldn't understand why all of a sudden he was giving her the cold shoulder. When he finally explained himself, Hannah caved in and apologised for her behaviour and agreed to going clothes shopping with Samuel for him to buy her some new loose blouses.

Whilst in the shop Samuel pointed out to Hannah a woman with large breasts wearing a vest top and showing quite a bit of cleavage. Samuel told Marsha that the woman's breasts where not even as large as hers and look how tarty she looked. Marsha tried to justify herself stating that at least she was not showing her cleavage. Marsha also tried to get Samuel to understand how difficult it was for her to get blouses and shirts that fit due to the size of her bust. It also came to Marsha's attention that Samuel was talking about and staring at the other woman's breasts long after their discussion. Marsha mentioned this to him as she felt somewhat offended; however, he instantly denied he was overly staring at the other woman.

Would you allow your partner to buy new blouses for you under these circumstances? What about him staring at the other woman's breasts for so long?

Marsha felt uncomfortable and she could not see anything that she really liked. Anything that she picked up, Samuel was not keen on. She became increasingly stressed and picked up three blouses, two of which she would not have bought for herself. Marsha ignored her intuition big time. She was bullied into wearing clothes that she did not like. Her intuition was screaming at her yet she ignored it. She did not put two and two together – Samuel was blatantly staring at this other woman's breast and clearly did not want anyone staring at Marsha's, hence why he wanted her to be wearing baggy blouses. He had a roving eye and at this stage Marsha had not yet picked up on it.

If you are easily controlled it is likely that you are co-dependent. This means that you put other people's feelings before your own; you tend to people please due to your lack of self-esteem. If your partner is controlling in one area of life, it is likely that he will control you in other areas. Control issues are quite deep rooted and it's a clear sign of trouble along the way. If this sounds familiar to you then I would suggest you explore these issues and perhaps seek professional help. Codependency is deep rooted and often stems from being brought up in a dysfunctional family.

10 FAMILY AND FRIENDS

When you have a partner it is only natural to meet their family and friends at some point. It is vital that you meet them as you get to know a bit more about your partner, this in turn helps you make more of an informed choice as to whether you want to develop a serious relationship with them. When I was a young girl my mother used to say to me "Show me your friends and I will tell you who you are". How very true this is. We all know the common phrase, bird of a feather flock together.

Getting to know your partners' family is also very important as again, it gives you a sense of who they are. You cannot necessarily judge your partner by their family; because they may have done work on themselves to overcome their issues if they came from a dysfunctional family. However, it does give you an idea of where they are coming from.

Marsha talked about how her partner Samuel did not introduce her to any of his friends. He went as far to say that he doesn't really have any good friends; despite the fact that he occasionally met up with one or two. However, he often spoke about his friends to her, mentioning how awful they were when it came to women and the sorts of things they would get up to when they were younger. Marsha was not impressed and even questioned Samuel about some of the things he spoke about. Naturally Samuel said he was different, he didn't agree with what they did. For this reason, he did not want Marsha anywhere near them for he felt they would be inappropriate towards her.

What are you thinking? Are alarm bells ringing for you?

Hannah often complained to me that Andrew refused to introduce her to his family. He spoke about how dysfunctional his family was and he did not want her anywhere near them. He often talked about how awful they treated him as the last born of his family and he did not want her to be anywhere near them for fear they may be rude towards her. Hannah recalls on quite a few occasions that she would be waiting in the car for him whilst he went to visit his sister to pick up mail from her house (he had certain letters going there). Hannah could not understand his thinking and often questioned him; he would give small promises of how he would take her to meet his sister, however, he would coach her on how she should behave once they got there. Those visits never materialized. He often used the excuse that his family were messed up and didn't like strangers in their house. In fact when Hannah would question him about this he would become very angry turning it around on her saying that she was not being understanding. In the end Hannah would end up feeling bad and apologising even though she had a nagging feeling that he was hiding something about him and his past.

What is going through your mind right now? What would you have done in this situation?

It is clear to see that both of these men had something to hide. Both Marsha and Hannah, were not using their intuition and ended up realizing that their men were not who they thought they were. Their men pulled the wool over their eyes. So it is very important to know where your partner is coming from.

Better to know as early as possible for fear that later down the line you discover that they are not who you thought they were. Some people lead double lives; Andrew and Samuel's behaviour are an indication that they were probably leading double lives.

11 DO YOUR CHILDREN LIKE HIM?

Children are extremely intuitive because they are closer to source energy. They see auras; feel energies a lot more than most adults. Many people talk of how their children see family members that have passed away. Sometimes what may appear to be a nightmare for a child could well be someone from the spirit world, and again it all depends on the parents' beliefs how these experiences are perceived and interpreted.

I remember as a young child when my mother brought a man home who was interested in her to meet us. I did not like him, I don't know why but I just did not like him. It's often difficult for children to explain why they don't like certain adults. The problem is that most adults think that their child is just being indignant. They sometimes believe that their child is jealous because this new man may take their mother away from them. This may be the case in some instances but often it is because the child or children can sense the persons' energies. They often have a sense of 'knowing' and we would do well to give our children some credit.

Going back to when I was a young child and this man that my mother brought home, he ended up going off with my mother's tenant who stayed in our house. Naturally my mother was upset, however, I and my siblings were not. Now, many years later this man came back into my mother's life and I got the same feeling as I did when I was a child. I was now 18 years old and really did not take to this man whatsoever. In fact, all of my siblings felt the same way and there was a lot of tension within the whole family. Fights, arguments ensued and it was not pretty. My mother ended up marrying this man. A few years down the line he managed to molest my daughter when she was in my mother's care. This was probably one of the most devastating experiences of my life. Because I tried to accept him for my mother's sake ignoring what my intuition felt about him. So even as a child my intuition was correct.

My children were not that keen on my ex-partner but made the effort to get on with him. Although I sensed that he did not make much of an effort with them, especially my son, who was the main one that felt he was not good for me. I half listened to my children and now wished I fully listened to them. They were right about him. Children are very protective of their mums and it is important for us to acknowledge and respect that in them. My children started to feel very uncomfortable in their own home due to the amount of time he was spending with me, with him staying over for most nights in the week. They spoke about wanting to move out because the house was too small and they felt claustrophobic. Yes our home was small, but they did not complain like that before and I often felt that they were just being difficult.

When I finally ended the relationship I did some spiritual rituals of lighting white candles in the home, burning incense and made sure I gave him back all of his property. All of this was to ensure that his energy was no longer present in my home. Something I had noticed towards the end of the relationship was that he tended to drain my energy when I was around him. It was bizarre and I could not understand what that was about at the time. My children did not know why I was lighting these candles. But a few weeks after the split they said that the house feels different now that I had split up with him. They did not feel the need to move out anymore. They felt more comfortable in their home. I was a little gob smacked to say the least.

So, will you listen to your children? Can you think of occasions in the past where your children have spoken, 'acted out' and you ignored them only to find later on that they were right?

PART 3

12 PERSONAL DEVELOPMENT

This is why I am so passionate about personal development. We are not here to stand still. The universe is constantly changing. Nothing is supposed to stay the same. So why would we expect to stay the same as we were last year? If you are feeling dissatisfied with your life, it could be that it is time to take a look inwards.

What do you feel is missing in your life?

Where would you like to be or what would you like to be doing in five years' time, or even ten years' time?

How do you really feel about change, be honest with yourself?

I would like you to really consider the above questions and in the space provided write out your answers.

Imagine yourself in a small circle and as you stand in that circle you see beyond it so many different things that you do not know, yet you feel curious about. Take a small step outside of that circle and go on a trip to investigate what is beyond the realms of your circle. This is the first step to transformation and stepping out of your comfort zone. If your life has felt comfortable for a long time then it is time to step out of your comfort zone. This is where transformation happens. If you then start to feel uncomfortable this is a good thing because it means you are transforming.

Every person is different and has their way of dealing with change.

- Some resist it until the last minute when they feel forced to make changes.
- Some have changed thrust upon them and they have no choice but to deal with change.
- Others still, will be slightly curious and watch others around them changing and feel that they too need to change in order to keep up.
- Then you get those stubborn ones who refuse to change, they become stagnant, bitter and are really quite negative and judgemental of others.

Which one are you?

How will you move forward from now?

It could be something very small to start off with, something you know you can keep up with. Stepping out of your comfort zone is uncomfortable, however this is a sign that the changes you are making are working. The more changes you make the more you will transform your life.

We are the creators of our own reality, so what reality are you creating for yourself? Do you find that what you want is not what you are getting in life? For example, do you want a life partner with all the attributes that will make them that special someone; and do you find you are attracted to or are attracting a different type of person, someone without those special attributes? If so, then something is surely amiss. The answer is, your subconscious mind is leading the show. Yes, your subconscious mind plays a very big part in creating our reality and if you find your reality isn't what your conscious mind is asking for then you have work to do. Yes, work to do on releasing whatever is blocking you from having the life you want.

Your subconscious mind is where all your limiting beliefs and core beliefs lie. In order to get to it, you will need to start on your journey of self-discovery to remove those limiting and negative core beliefs that are holding you back. You will need to release any trauma that is locked in your mid brain. It is only then that you will start to notice the difference. Yes it may seem scary, but what is worse, living a life that you hate or going through a temporary period of discomfort in order to pave the way for you to live the life of your dreams? Yes your dreams can come true, but it's down to you to make it happen.

13 WHERE THE MAGIC HAPPENS

We are spiritual beings living a human existence and as such we are limitless. We have been conditioned to believe otherwise. However, once we start to embrace our true selves we will come to the realisation that we are in fact geniuses. Clearing your subconscious of all debris, issues, limiting beliefs, emotional baggage is the best thing you can do for yourselves because once it is cleared you will then be highly attuned. You will be more connected to source, your higher self, God, the universe. Whichever description suits you they all mean the same thing.

Once connected your intuition will grow, it will become stronger and you will feel so empowered. You will be on a spiritual high and know that you can achieve whatever you put your mind to. This connection is where true happiness lies because your higher self is always and has always been happy. It's the part of you that is at one with the universe.

Close your eyes; sit quietly for a while and imagine being connected to source and how that would feel for you. Write your feelings here.

What sort of life would you create for yourself? Really use your imagination here and dream big dreams.

So this is why I stress the importance of clearing yourself of 'stuff'. This is what is holding you back from manifesting the life you so desire. This is what stops you from having a positive mindset. This is what hinders you from being truly happy. This is why you cannot operate on a high vibration.

In order to manifest your true desires you need to be operating on a high frequency vibration that is full of love and positivity. This vibration is what makes us happy, wealthy, successful, and healthy.

How much longer will you put off releasing your 'stuff'?

What stops you?

For most people fear is what stops them. Did you know that fear means one or more of the following?

- **F**alse **E**xpectations **A**ppearing **R**eal
- **F**ace **E**verything **A**nd **R**ecover
- **F***** **E**verything **A**nd **R**un

Which one will you pick?

Susan Jeffers says we need to feel the fear and do it anyway. Yes feeling fear is part of our makeup but our fear is misguided because it is not meant to stop us from progressing in life. It is only there to protect us from danger. Our 'stuff' that we carry isn't going to cause us any real danger if we deal with it. We unconsciously know that letting go of our stuff is likely to cause us pain. But I can assure you it will not be as painful as the actual thing we experienced in the past. The pain will not last forever, it too shall pass.

How much longer do you want to be suffering, struggling, being unhappy, feeling unfulfilled? One of the worst things we could do is have regrets. Surely you would not want to leave this earthly plane having had regrets that you did not live your life to the fullest.

Have you actually answered the questions in the book? Did you write in the spaces provided, or did you just bypass the questions? How serious are you about your personal development? Did you know that writing is a very powerful therapeutic aid? So I urge you to use the space and start writing and once you have finished reading this book, continue to journal about your feelings, experiences, as well as your goals and aspirations.

14 EMBRACE YOURSELF

Be Authentic - What does it mean to be authentic? To authenticate something means making it genuine, or the real deal. Are you being authentic? Are you being real, are you being true to you. In essence, are you portraying the real deal of who you are?

It can be a challenge to be authentic because we fear that if people see the real you they may not even like you. Why should you care if people like you? Do you like you? If you like yourself, your true self, that's all that counts isn't it? If you do not like your true self, then what is it about yourself that you do not like? Is it something that you can change, for example a flaw in your character; something that you can develop? If so, then that isn't so much of a problem is it? You can change it. If it is something that you cannot change, for example, your height, your build then learn to accept it and love it. Learn to accept yourself with all your warts; as you are right now. That does not mean you cannot work on making positive changes in your life, but focus on loving you for who you are right now.

If people do not like you, don't worry, they'll hate you more when you become brilliant, or the person you were born to be. It is none of your business if others don't like you, because by focusing on what others think of you is what holds you back from being real. There will be many others that will like you for who you really are.

I love what Marianne Williamson says and I think it is very powerful. Do read the following and really digest her words:

"Our deepest fear is not that we are inadequate, our deepest fear is that we are powerful beyond measure. It is our light, not our darkness, that most frightens us. We ask ourselves: 'Who am I to be brilliant, gorgeous, talented, fabulous?' Actually, who are you not to be? You are a child of God. Your playing small doesn't serve the world. There is nothing enlightening about shrinking so that other people around you won't feel insecure. We are all meant to shine as

children do. We are born to manifest the glory of God that is within us. It is not just in some of us; it is in everyone. And as we let our light shine, we unconsciously give other people permission to do the same. As we are liberated from our own fear, our presence automatically liberates others." (Marianne Williamson)

Did you know that many people out there can spot a fake person? For some people it is quite easy to do so, just as easy as spotting a fake Louis Vuitton bag, probably even easier. Is that what you want? People do not like to be around a fake person. Other descriptions for fake are bogus, replica, imitation; surely you would not want to be seen as that and certainly you would prefer people to see the real you and know that you are being genuine. What's the worst thing that can happen by being authentic? Do not be afraid to let your true self shine through. Take off the mask and reveal your inner beauty, your inner soul, your greatness. Life then becomes less of a struggle.

What aspects of yourself you love?

It is very important that a woman learns to embrace herself. Self-acceptance is the key to many things and when we learn to accept who we are as a woman we are onto a good thing. As a woman, you have many roles in society. A mother, daughter, niece, auntie, lover, wife, some of us are grandmothers. In addition, we are workers and depending on the type of job that you do, you will use different aspects of your womanly nature to perform your job.

Some of us work in the caring profession and this is where your nurturing side will come into play. Of the two species women are the nurturers (well most of us are). This aspect of our make-up helps us to look after our babies; it also serves us in our romantic relationships. Men love to be nurtured and indeed need some nurturing. However, we want to be careful that we do not mother our men, they have a mother or had a mother and as such we need to be careful not to get mixed up with our role as their lover or wife. If a man expects you to mother him, then he has issues and needs to seek some professional help or embark on some personal development. If you find that you tend to mother your man, then you also have issues and likewise need to seek professional help and embark on some personal development.

Embrace your womanly qualities without fear of judgment – your sensual side and sexual side. As well as being a spiritual being you are also a sexual being, a loving being. We are beings with forms of expression. Do not be afraid to express each aspect of who you are. Do not hold onto any shame around expressing yourself as a sexual being. If there is shame, then it's likely you need to work on your views around sex and resolve any issues you may have about that. I am not advocating slack behaviour as highlighted in the media, but merely saying that to express yourself sexually freely without fear of being judged is a truly wonderful feeling.

Expressions of love are also remarkable. We are love. When you truly learn to love yourself first and foremost then the rest is easy. For many people loving self is a bit of a task, especially those coming from dysfunctional families and society in general with its media really doesn't help us to love and accept ourselves. However, the more you work on loving self the happier you will become. Giving love without expecting anything in return heals our spiritual problems and receiving love heals our soul problems. In order to have a healthy equilibrium give love and be open to receiving love. Know that you are capable of giving and worthy of receiving. You are loving and you are loveable. Love is the greatest quality there is and next to joy creates the best feelings one can ever imagine.

****

When the power of women comes together untold blessings will befall the world. It will bring about massive change. Women will nurture men and they will eventually stop trying to dominate. The world is changing. Discrimination in its many forms will start to fade away as the earths' consciousness changes for the greater good of humanity. When you trust your intuition you do a good thing. This is the seat of empowerment. This is how you empower yourself. It speaks to you constantly. It's a powerful part of you. It is there for a reason and it will guide you to safety, guide you to the right people. You must learn to trust yourself, it is essential for the survival of the human race. It goes far beyond you; listening to your intuition when it comes to meeting men and other people in your life is imperative. As you learn to trust it you will start to evolve where you just know what to do, what to say etc.

Can you imagine how free that will make you feel?

No more second guessing, no more doubting yourself and no more time wasted on certain individuals who mean you no good. Drink from the cup of the divine one because you too are divine.

****

MY ANSWERS TO THE QUESTIONS

CHAPTER 5

How long do you wait for the call? One, two, three days… one week; two weeks? Would you have called him?

3 days

Do you agree with what Marsha had done? What would you have done? Would you have questioned him as to why he doesn't drive?

I agree with Marsha, I would not go into his flat as it is only the first date, I don't know him that well. I would also ask him why he doesn't drive, just so I know the situation because there are many reasons – he could be banned, he could be in between cars, his car could be in the garage etc. PS. I would have called him up and cancelled the date – 2 hours late is totally unacceptable.

CHAPTER 6

How would you have handled the situation?

I would not get stroppy. I would point out to him that my time is precious and that I don't do lateness. I would wait only for 10 minutes for him, and expect a phone call to say he is running late.

Should she have accepted his lateness, should it have taken so long to come to a compromise?

I would not have accepted this, it wouldn't develop into a relationship for it to be a regular occurrence; i.e. if it happened three times I would not wish to see him again.

What would you have done?

I would get on with my life. If I heard from him any time after the said time I would tell him that I am no longer interested and wish him well. If it was due to an emergency, I would send my sympathies and still wish him well. Even in an emergency to make a phone or send a text is not that difficult.

Would you have gone out without him, or would you have sacrificed your night out and gone to his house?

I would still go out with my friend as planned and call him the following day to see how he is doing.

Would you be feeling guilty too?

No, as I have nothing to feel guilty about.

What should Hannah have done? What would you have done?

Hannah should have gone home straight from the club. The fact that he did not answer his phone says one of two things, either he is genuinely sick and sleeping, thus needing his rest, or he is sulking and deliberately not answering his phone. Either way, I certainly would not have made my way there. If he didn't answer the phone when I rang him from the club, I would stay with my friend and continue to enjoy my night out. I would then call him in the morning to see how he is.

Would you have ignored it and given him the benefit of the doubt?

If my intuition felt it I would not ignore it; despite the fact that he could have been telling the truth.

What are you thinking? Do you agree?

I agree, there is no need to rush, however, if we agree on a time I expect that agreement to be met, unless something urgent comes up, in which case I would expect a phone call.

Do you agree with Samuel? What would you have said to Samuel if it were you?

I do not agree with Samuel. It is clear that Marsha has had enough of the constant lateness and has every right to be annoyed. She should have spoken about it in an adult fashion and told Samuel this. If he felt disrespected I would tell him that I also felt disrespected by him not honoring my time. However, for me, Samuel would have been shown the door long before things got to this point.

Would you have done the same, if not what would you have done differently?

I would not be apologising. I would tell him that I am no longer prepared to put up with the constant lateness. Forget about the night out and end the relationship.

CHAPTER 7

What are you thinking right now about what he said? Do you sense anything?

I am thinking that this man has no intention of marrying me; which is fine, as I have already been married twice. However, I am sensing something else, which is making me wonder how does he view this relationship, and me?

What would you have thought if your partner had made that joke to you, about you?

I would believe what he said and would not pursue the relationship. In fact, I would be none too pleased to be viewed in that way as I think it is quite disrespectful.

CHAPTER 8

What are your views on how a man talks about his ex?

For me, to talk about the mother of your children in such a way is unacceptable. In fact, to view women in such a way is a warped view as the majority of women do not behave in a whorish fashion and if they do, it is likely that there are serious deep rooted issues that they clearly need to address.

CHAPTER 9

What do you think of the above situation? Would you have said anything? Would you have accepted the dresses?

I think there is a fundamental difference in what we consider to be decent. Not only that, I sense he wants to control the way I dress and as a grown woman that is not really acceptable. Even though I liked the dresses, the new me would not have accepted those dresses. I would also make it clear that I wear what I want and if he has an issue with that he would have to deal with it or not.

Would you allow your partner to buy new blouses for you under these circumstances? What about him staring at the other woman's breasts for so long?

I would not allow my partner to buy me the blouses under those circumstances. I see it as caving in under his control and I will not be controlled. As for him staring at the other woman's bust, if that is what I saw him doing it would raise alarm bells that he likely has a roving eye. In addition, to be doing that in front of me I would find totally disrespectful. That being said, I would choose not to be in a relationship with such a man.

CHAPTER 10

What are you thinking? Are alarm bells ringing for you?

I am thinking that birds of a feather flock together, and the fact that he does not want me around them is confirming to me that something is amiss. Alarm bells are definitely ringing. If he has no 'real' friends, that again is saying a lot to me. I am feeling that I cannot trust this person as it feels like he has something to hide.

What is going through your mind right now? What would you have done in this situation?

Right now, I am thinking this man is clearly hiding something especially for him to get angry with me for bringing it up on occasion. This would have led me to not wanting to be in a relationship with him because if I sense someone is trying to hide something from me then there is not enough openness within the relationship. This kind of relationship is doomed.

The remaining questions are your own personal dreams, aspirations and goals, hence my answers end here.

ABOUT THE AUTHOR

Yvonne J Douglas' purpose and passion is to inspire, empower and motivate individuals to reach their highest potential. She does this through her multidisciplinary skills and talents. A dynamic individual who just by her aura can change the people she comes into contact with. Yvonne is the proud mother of two young adults, whom she brought up on her own, guiding and encouraging them to take charge of their lives.

Yvonne has become an extremely empowered individual due to her tenacity, courage and determination to heal herself. She is dedicated in helping others heal from past hurts, pain and traumas.

Yvonne's private practice aims to provide an exemplary service to enable individuals to face their fears and release their emotional baggage in order to become the success they have always dreamt of. Yvonne prides herself in making people successful in all areas of life and endeavors to lead by example.

Issues that Yvonne can help with include addictions, phobias, anxiety, depression, trauma, sexual abuse, emotional issues, and low self-esteem and relationship problems, moving you through change enabling you to tap into your most powerful self and achieving magnificent results.

Yvonne has been recognised by Worldwide Who's Who for her counselling achievements in November 2011. In July 2012 Yvonne was chosen as an inspirational figure within the Black 100+ legacy book, in addition, she was selected as one of the top 50 inspirational and international people by the Swanilenga Group Ltd. She has been on numerous radio shows talking about her experiences and her books. Yvonne plans to go global with her public speaking as she is currently one of the most inspirational speakers in the UK. For more information on Yvonne please visit www.yvonnejdouglas.com or www.onenessofspirit.co.uk

Other books by Yvonne J Douglas:

Hungry for Love

Go For It - It's Your Life

Yvonne J Douglas

Made in the USA
Charleston, SC
11 January 2014